CLIMATE CHANGE

Erosion

By Shai Ivey

Mamu

COUNTRY CULTURE COMMUNITY

We respect and honour Aboriginal and Torres Strait Islander Elders past, present and future. We acknowledge the stories, traditions and living cultures of Aboriginal and Torres Strait Islander peoples on this land and commit to building a brighter future together.

Library For All Ltd.

What is Erosion?

Erosion in waterways happens when water, especially during extreme tides, flooding, and rising sea levels, moves soil and rocks from the riverbanks. Scientists study how these events change river dynamics, such as increasing the water flow and altering the river's shape and sediment distribution.

Erosion can be very dangerous and even deadly!

Erosion affects not only the land but also the plants, animals, and the people who depend on it for survival. Erosion can be a natural process, but climate change has quickened it to the point of danger.

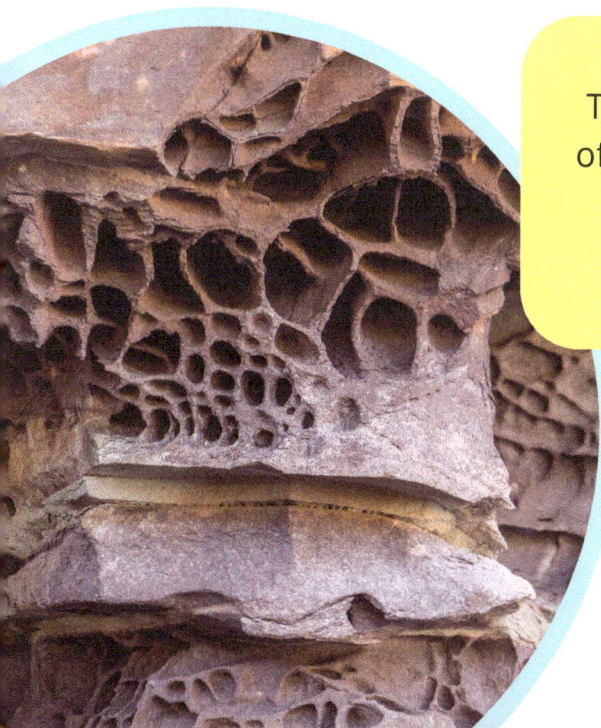

The four main types of erosion are: water, friction, wind and chemical.

How Erosion Impacts Riverbanks

Layers of soil and rock being washed away by erosion makes the ground unstable. It can also destroy fertile land, making it impossible to grow food on.

Native plants play a crucial role against erosion because their roots hold soil together, preventing it from being washed away. It's their role to stabilise riverbanks during extreme weather.

DID YOU KNOW?

Climate change increases flooding and sea levels, threatening to worsen erosion.

Erosion, Riverbanks, and Indigenous Knowledge

Indigenous communities are severely affected by the erosion of riverbanks due to the long history of communities relying on these ecosystems to live. Indigenous communities have developed some traditional practices for stabilising riverbanks and preventing erosions.

Erosion causes landslides, worsened flooding, and unfertile farmland.

A primary practice is planting native vegetation with deep root systems.

Native Plants and Erosion

Certain native trees and grasses are vital for stabilising riverbanks. The grasses that best combat erosion change region-to-region, mainly due to the differing weather patterns throughout Australia.

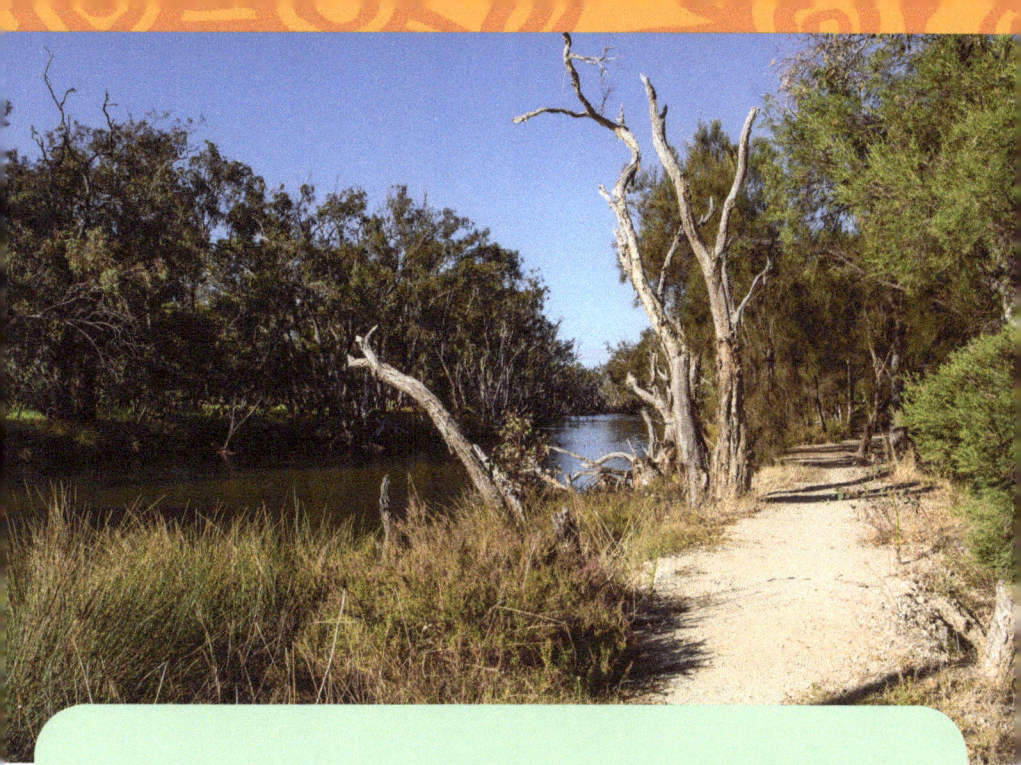

Many native plants' roots grow deep and wide, holding the soil together, and help to maintain the river's existing shape during floods instead of allowing it to expand.

Even beyond keeping erosion at bay, native plants also provide habitats for wildlife and contribute to the overall health of the ecosystem. This health works against erosion too, making the land harder to displace.

Eroded riverbanks can be risky to walk on or play near. Always be mindful of things in the water and the ground breaking underfoot, and the risk of drowning.

Conservation on Eroded Areas

What do we do?

Conservation efforts focus on planting native plants, which are effective at stabilising riverbanks, and implementing measures to protect these areas from further erosion. These further measures include controlling water runoff and protecting vulnerable soils with covers.

Using the land correctly is also important for preventing erosion.

Cultural Views on Riverbanks

Riverbanks and native plants are often regarded with reverence and respect in Indigenous cultures, and are seen as sacred entities that sustain life and embody the spirit of the land.

Views on Native Plants

Native plants growing along the riverbanks have been utilised by Indigenous people for thousands of years as food, medicine, shelter, tools, and ceremonial purposes. These uses are passed down through traditional knowledge from generation to generation.

Traditional knowledge includes understanding the properties and uses of various plant species, as well as sustainable harvesting practices that ensure they continue to grow.

Ongoing Conservation

Modern conservation practices include planting native plants, building barriers to slow down water flow, and creating safe spaces for excess water during floods, extreme tides, and rising sea levels.

Protecting riverbanks from erosion is an ever-evolving job. There's always new technology and ideas to help conserve these vital spaces.

Traditional Riverbank Protection Practices

After flood events, Indigenous communities often engage in revegetation efforts using native plant species. Seeds, cuttings, or saplings of native plants are collected and replanted along the riverbank to stabilise soil to prevent erosion and restore habitats for the wildlife.

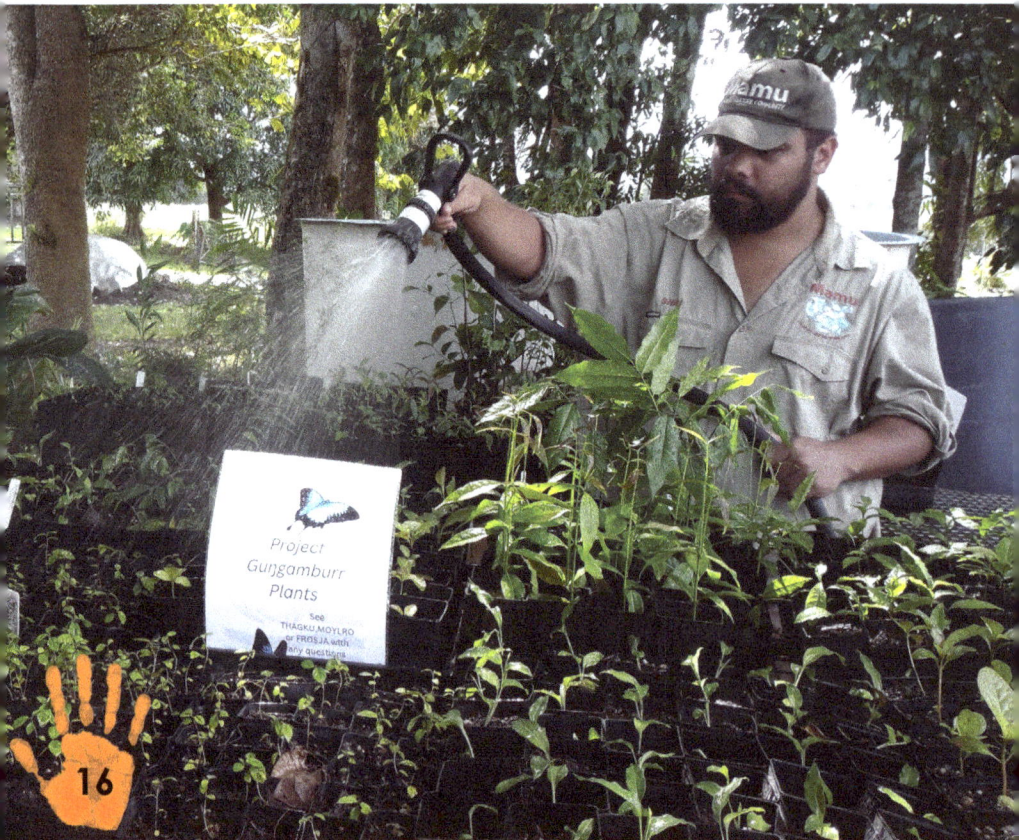

Riverbanks are also important homes to animals!

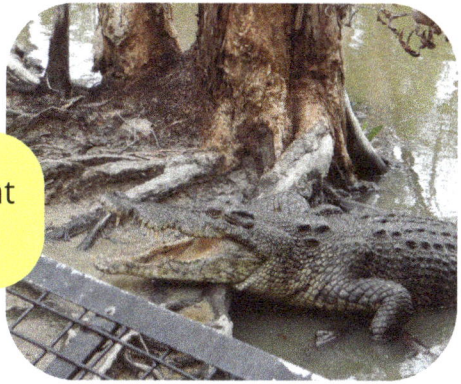

Indigenous knowledge guides the selection of appropriate plant species that are well adapted to local environmental conditions. This sort of knowledge is why incorporating Indigenous practices into modern riverbank protection plans is the best way to preserve the land.

DID YOU KNOW?

Animals live along riverbanks for many reasons. Platypuses need the water for swimming, while others like the koala need it to drink.

Did You know?

Native Plants and Riverbanks

Some native plants can thrive both in water and on dry land, making them ideal for stabilising riverbanks. These plants can slow down water flow, spread it out, and help reduce the impact of flooding, extreme tides, and erosion. Planting several different species is the best course of action.

Many native plants used for stabilising riverbanks have intricate root structures that go beyond merely anchoring soil. Some species, like certain sedges and grasses, have fibrous roots that create a dense network. Others, like the willows and cotton wood, develop deep taproots that can penetrate several metres in the ground.

Photo Credits

Page	Attribution
Cover	Genevieve Vallee/Alamy Stock Photo
Page 2	Eric Krouse/Shutterstock.com
Page 3 (above)	corlaffra/Shutterstock.com
Page 3 (below)	robertharding / Alamy Stock Photo
Pages 4–5	Jason Knott / Alamy Stock Photio
Pages 6–7	Photo courtesy of the Queensland Indigenous Land and Sea Ranger Program.
Page 8	BeautifulBlossoms/Shutterstock.com
Page 9	ciw1/Shutterstock.com
Page 10	© Library For All
Page 11	Photo courtesy of the Queensland Indigenous Land and Sea Ranger Program.
Page 12	Genevieve Vallee / Alamy Stock Photo
Page 13	Photo courtesy of the Queensland Indigenous Land and Sea Ranger Program.
Page 14-15	Keith Mecklem/Shutterstock.com
Page 15 (above)	Photo courtesy of the Queensland Indigenous Land and Sea Ranger Program.
Page 16	Photo courtesy of the Queensland Indigenous Land and Sea Ranger Program.
Page 17	Pascal Vosicki/Shutterstock.com
Page 18 (left)	Tammy27/Shutterstock.com
Page 18 (right)	Ralph Gillen/Shutterstock.com
Page 19	tkatasila/Shutterstock.com

You can use these questions to talk about this book with your family, friends and teachers.

What did you learn from this book?

Describe this book in one word. Funny? Scary? Colourful? Interesting?

How did this book make you feel when you finished reading it?

What was your favourite part of this book?

Queensland Indigenous Land and Sea Ranger Program

The Queensland Indigenous Land and Sea Ranger Program collaborates with First Nations communities to protect and care for land and sea Country. With over 200 rangers, the program shares cultural knowledge, engages in community education, and leads youth programs like the Junior Ranger initiative, fostering a strong connection to Country and Culture.

Shai Ivey is a Mamu Ranger from the Innisfail community.

Our Yarning

The Our Yarning collection aligns with the Australian Curriculum through the Cross-Curriculum Priorities — Aboriginal and Torres Strait Islander Histories and Cultures. The collection provides an authentic opportunity for learning and embedding Aboriginal and Torres Strait Islander perspectives because it is written by Aboriginal and Torres Strait Islander people.

We know that children learn better, and enjoy reading more, when they see themselves in the stories, characters and illustrations of the books they read.

To download the app, visit the Google Play Store or Apple Store and search 'Our Yarning'.

libraryforall.org

You're reading Upper Primary

Learner – Beginner readers

Start your reading journey with short words, big ideas and plenty of pictures.

Level 1 – Rising readers

Raise your reading level with more words, simple sentences and exciting images.

Level 2 – Eager readers

Enjoy your reading time with familiar words, but complex sentences.

Level 3 – Progressing readers

Develop your reading skills with creative stories and some challenging vocabulary.

Level 4 – Fluent readers

Step up your reading skills with playful narratives, new words and fun facts.

Middle Primary – Curious readers

Discover your world through science and stories.

Upper Primary – Adventurous readers

Explore your world through science and stories.

Library For All is an Australian not for profit organisation with a mission to make knowledge accessible to all via an innovative digital library solution.
Visit us at libraryforall.org

Climate Change: Erosion

First published 2024

Published by Library For All Ltd
Email: info@libraryforall.org
URL: libraryforall.org

This project was delivered with the support of QBE under the Community Ready partnership.

Community Ready

This book was made possible with the support of the Queensland Indigenous Land and Sea Ranger Program to support educational outcomes for children in Australia by learning from Indigenous knowledge and stewardship of Country. To learn more, visit https://www.qld.gov.au/environment/plants-animals/conservation/community/land-sea-rangers/locations.

Queensland Indigenous Land and Sea Rangers

Queensland Government

Our Yarning logo design by Jason Lee, Bidjipidji Art

Climate Change: Erosion
Ivey, Shai
ISBN: 978-1-923207-49-3
SKU04436

www.ingramcontent.com/pod-product-compliance
Lightning Source LLC
Chambersburg PA
CBHW042343040426
42448CB00019B/3388